Contents

The power of print

'*I READ IT IN THE PAPER.*' That short statement says a lot about the role of newspapers and magazines in our lives. It shows how printed words can influence the way we behave and even how we think. Newspapers can inspire people to give to worthy causes, to honour the memory of soldiers who fought for freedom, or to protest against laws that seem cruel or unfair. But the sentence above says something even more dramatic – that what I read is true because it was in the newspaper.

Newspaper readers in China can choose from a growing number of titles, but the government still influences what appears in print.

GETTING THE
MESSAGE

Newspapers and Magazines

How to interpret
what we see, read and hear

Sean Connolly

W

FRANKLIN WATTS
LONDON•SYDNEY

An Appleseed Editions book

First published in 2009 by Franklin Watts
338 Euston Road, London NW1 3BH

Franklin Watts Australia
Hachette Children's Books
Level 17/207 Kent St, Sydney, NSW 2000

Created by Appleseed Editions Ltd,
Well House, Friars Hill, Guestling,
East Sussex TN35 4ET

Designed by Helen James
Edited by Mary-Jane Wilkins
Picture research by Su Alexander

ISBN 978 07496 8779 3

Dewey Classification: 302.23' 2

A CIP catalogue for this book is available from the British Library.

Photograph acknowledgements
page 6 Bohemian Nomad Picturemakers/Corbis; 9 Bettmann/Corbis; 10 Getty Images;
12 Reuters/Corbis; 14 Bettmann/Corbis; 16 Hulton-Deutsch Collection/Corbis;
19 Chris Collins/Corbis; 20 Bettmann/Corbis; 22 I.T.N./Rex Features; 24 Fiona
Hanson/PA Archive/PA Photos; 26 PA/PA Archive/PA Photos; 28 & 30 Bettmann/
Corbis; 32 Ali Jarekji/Reuters/Corbis; 34 Yevgeny Khaldei/Corbis; 37 Tannen Maury/
EPA/Corbis; 38 Getty Images; 40 Jock Lauterer; 42 Alan Towse; Ecoscene/Corbis
Front cover Bohemian Nomad Picturemakers/Corbis

Printed in China

Franklin Watts is a division of Hachette Children's Books,
an Hachette Livre UK company.
www.hachettelivre.co.uk

Seeing something in print, rather than just hearing the same fact, changes the way people respond to it. In the same way, people often refer to a particular newspaper as being their 'bible' or their 'gospel'. Again, it is the power of the printed word that is stressed. Many Christians believe that everything they need to know is found within the pages of the Bible. For them, the Bible is nothing less than the sacred word of God, preserved on the printed page for all time and for everyone. It is hardly surprising that some of these people might transfer this respect for the written word to the newspapers and magazines they read.

Wider issues

There would be no place for this book if everyone agreed that newspapers and magazines are a force for good – that they provide an opportunity for unbiased people to report events accurately for the general good of the world.

The truth is far more complicated. Think of an issue about which people disagree, such as whether the prime minister is doing a good job – and then look at how a range of newspapers and magazines deal with the issue. There is usually a lot of disagreement, and some of the criticism – of political leaders, sports stars and celebrities – can be strongly worded.

This book examines why the same story can be told in many different – and contradictory – ways. Some of the reasons are easy enough to understand or even to guess. But behind the obvious answers are subtler questions, about the role of money, power, religion and government – and the way that some people would like to turn the precious freedom of the press to their own advantage.

In the know

People have always been curious about what is going on in the wider world. That world might be a local neighbourhood or village, or it could encompass the whole of the known world. The information people absorb is considered news whether it is the announcement of changed opening hours at the local library or information about a space probe sent to explore Mars.

Early news reports

One of the first printed accounts of news goes back to the time of ancient Rome, more than 2000 years ago. Julius Caesar ordered that a printed account of important matters, *Acta Diurna* (meaning daily events), be posted throughout the city. Interested Romans could read about destructive fires, public executions or devastating storms. By the early eighth century the Chinese government was collecting reports of events in a publication called the *Kai Yuan Za Bao*. Copies were printed on silk using woodblocks and then distributed to government officials throughout the Chinese empire.

Hundreds of years later in the early 1400s, Europeans could read newsletters telling them about events in different parts of the continent. Representatives of rich European merchants sent these handwritten letters back to their home cities, where they were circulated and widely read. But although these newsletters contained a great deal of new information about the world at large, they cannot be considered to be newspapers.

The printed word

The development of the printing press in the late 1400s revolutionized the way people gathered information – including news of the wider world. By the seventeenth century, the Germans and Dutch were leading

Londoners in the 1700s met in coffee houses to discuss the news and gossip appearing in the latest newspapers.

the way in producing what we now call newspapers. These publications appeared daily or weekly, and presented a mixture of political news and scandal. The mixture often landed editors in trouble with the government or church officials.

The English seized on this exciting mixture of news and gossip. The first English-language daily newspaper, the *Daily Courant*, first appeared in 1702. It was printed above the White Hart pub in Fleet Street, London. Fleet Street gradually became the centre of the English newspaper industry. By the nineteenth century, people used the phrase Fleet Street to describe the industry as a whole. Even in the twenty-first century, when most British newspapers have moved elsewhere, the term is still used.

The nineteenth century saw an outpouring of new magazines, which might be published weekly, fortnightly or monthly. Unlike newspapers, which sought out the largest readership possible, magazines were devoted to special interests such as science, religion, fashion, or more detailed study of politics. Divisions between newspaper and magazines were blurred, and often depended on how often a publication came out. Some newspapers of the time, including the *Observer* and *The Times*, ran stories that matched magazine articles in length.

The modern age

Newspapers and magazines reflected the world around them through the nineteenth and early twentieth centuries – reporting on wars and national politics, natural disasters and new plays. But although the subject matter changed to reflect the modern world, the publications themselves were produced with methods that had hardly changed since the later eighteenth century.

The second half of the twentieth century shook up the industry. New printing techniques came in and it became cheaper and easier to print good-quality colour photographs. Newspapers reduced the number of people they employed as they found that machines (especially computers) could do much of the work. All these changes underlined an important point about newspapers and magazines: although most pride themselves on informing the public and spreading information, unless they make money they will go out of business.

Workers from The Times *and* Sunday Times *march along London's Fleet Street towards the* Times *buildings two months into the bitter dispute that led to the closure of both papers.*

SPOTLIGHT ON
No more Times

Well into the 1970s, British newspapers and magazines continued to be produced using methods that had been abandoned in many other parts of the world. Trade unions marked clear boundaries about which employees could do which jobs – and there was no room for overlap. For example, journalists could not directly type their stories into the typesetting machines; only members of a printers' union could do that.

By late 1978, the Thomson Organisation (owner of *The Times* and *Sunday Times*) had had enough of such rules – and the strikes that often arose because of them. Trying to force the unions to agree to new rules, Thomson actually closed both newspapers on 30 November 1978. They knew that this closure would reduce the company's profits, but Thomson felt that the unions would feel the loss sooner – and give in.

Instead the closure lasted weeks, and then months. In the end, it was not until mid-November 1979 – just hours before the deadline after which the owners had threatened permanent closure – when a deal was reached to bring the two newspapers back to the news-stands. Both sides claimed victory. The owners were able to get rid of 600 'unnecessary' jobs and to introduce some new equipment. They also won a promise from the unions not to stage unofficial strikes. The unions won better deals on holidays, pay and health benefits. They also kept the 'no journalists to type in stories' rule in place. That battle was to flare up again seven years later at *The Times*.

A newspaper makes money from the advertising space it sells in its pages, and also from the cover price – the price people pay to buy a copy. Raising the cover price makes the paper more money, provided that readers stay loyal to it. By reducing the cost of producing a newspaper, its owner can reduce the cover price. With luck, that lower price will attract more readers. And if the newspaper can then tell advertisers that more readers are noticing the ads, then the paper can charge more for those advertisements.

Gathering the news

Every edition of a newspaper or magazine is carefully planned. In charge of the whole operation is the editor, who must make sure that each member of the team knows exactly what to do, and when.

The different departments of a newspaper – such as home news, foreign news, business and sport – are called desks. Representatives of each desk join editorial meetings to decide which stories to include. The editor might also invite members of other departments to attend meetings, such as advertising. Nowadays, editorial meetings might include video or e-mail contributions from correspondents based in foreign cities.

Out in the field

When the main components of the next edition have been decided, reporters and photographers set out to gather the news. A lot of hard work goes into this – waiting around in bad weather for something to happen, interviewing people who might be angry or violent, going without food or sleep for days in a region affected by a natural disaster.

A reporter covering the Persian Gulf conflict in 1991 writes his story on a laptop while wearing special clothing to protect against poisonous gas attacks.

Tabloid journalism

In many countries, newspapers have traditionally been printed in two main sizes or formats – tabloid and broadsheet. Tabloid newspapers, regardless of their political views, usually have short, easy-to-follow news articles and lots of stories about entertainment and sport. Broadsheets take their name from the larger sheets of paper on which they are printed. They devote more space to news stories and articles discussing the background to events in the news. In addition to the difference in content, the two types of newspaper reflect very different approaches. Broadsheets aim to confine their political views to editorials and opinion-based articles which examine events in depth. They take pride in presenting their news stories accurately and fairly. But tabloids often make their political views clear throughout the paper. They also concentrate on the most extreme elements of the stories they report, sometimes making it hard for readers to form a balanced opinion about the subject.

Years ago, reporters sent their stories back to headquarters by telegraph, or returned to their desks to write them up. Nowadays reporters work on laptops and e-mail stories to their editors. They can also use mobile phones to dictate – or send shortened text versions of – their stories.

War reporting

One of the most controversial areas of journalism is war reporting. There is an old saying that truth is the first casualty when newspapers report on war. That is because governments – and many ordinary citizens – feel that it is disloyal to report when soldiers from your own country are cruel or suffer a heavy defeat. Of course, war reports may also tell positive news. During the worst days of the Second World War, many British readers were proud to read of the victories – as well as the occasional setbacks – of their armed forces.

Modern war reporting is now often carried out by reporters called embedded journalists. This is a direct result of the way the progress of the Vietnam War was reported during the 1970s. The war was the longest military conflict in US history, lasting from 1959 to 1975, and by the 1970s the US military had come to distrust the press. The war had become more and more unpopular in the US, largely because reporters depicted it as both unwinnable and wrong (see box right).

When the United States and other coalition countries invaded Iraq in 2003, the military embedded nearly 800 journalists and photographers. The journalists were allowed to live and travel with military units throughout the conflict, but had to sign contracts agreeing not to write about certain things. Lieutenant-Colonel Rick Long of the US Marines helped to shape this policy. A year after the invasion he defended it: 'Frankly, our job is to win the war. Part of that is information warfare. So we are going to attempt to dominate the information environment.'

Journalists are often on the front line in major conflicts. Japanese photographer Kyoichi Sawada won international awards for his photographs of the Vietnam War, but died in neighbouring Cambodia in 1970.

Two sides of the argument

The United States became involved in a long and costly war in the south-east Asian country of Vietnam from about 1960 until 1975. At one point, 500,000 American troops were based there, although the war became more and more unpopular at home. In 1975, North Vietnam defeated South Vietnam (the US ally) and united the formerly divided country.

War correspondent George C. Wilson was one of the American journalists who travelled halfway across the world to report on the Vietnam War in the 1960s. Forty years later, when soldiers from the United States and other coalition countries prepared to invade Iraq in 2003, Wilson was one of the hundreds of journalists assigned to the job.

As an embedded journalist, Wilson knew he would have constant access to a military unit, but that the military would also read what he reported. Unlike the military, he views the role of the press in Vietnam 35 years before as a triumph: 'I think Vietnam was one of the press's finest hours. They found out what was going on, they conveyed it to the people, people conveyed it to Congress, and Congress stopped the war by cutting off the money for it.'

Over to YOU

EDITOR'S CHOICE

IMAGINE YOU ARE THE EDITOR OF A NATIONAL NEWSPAPER AND YOU ARE DECIDING ON THE NEXT DAY'S LEAD STORY. YOU HAVE JUST CHOSEN TO LEAD WITH A STORY ABOUT THE RISING PRICE OF HOUSES WHEN A PHOTOGRAPHER COMES IN WITH PICTURES OF A DRUNKEN POLITICIAN PUNCHING A POLICEMAN. WOULD YOU CHANGE YOUR MIND AND CHOOSE THE STORY ABOUT THE POLITICIAN?

Going to press

Newspapers, magazines and other forms of written journalism are called the press. This term goes back to early printing technology. Print workers called typesetters or compositors had wooden cases full of individual metal letters, or type, from which they created words letter by letter – a laborious process. The letters were slotted into a block back to front, along with the punctuation, the spaces between the words and any rules between the columns of type.

Then the typesetter inked the finished block before placing the paper directly on the backward-reading page and pressing down so the ink would print the words on the paper the right way round.

PART OF A TEAM

Roger (not his real name) was a sub-editor on a political magazine during the 1980s. The magazine supported anti-war movements, environmental pressure groups and many other progressive issues. This is what he said about the experience. 'The people on the editorial team – from the editor to the sub-editors, picture researchers and reporters – came from all over the world. People had a great feeling working together for a cause they believed in, even if their governments were at odds with each other. I mean, we had an American guy and an Iranian woman working side by side.

'Feeling part of a team like that buried a lot of the tensions and rivalries that can crop up in magazines and newspapers. Normally, people in editorial have nothing to do with the advertising department; we figure that their main pleasure in life is to complain about the stuff we write. And I suppose they wonder why we run stories that will make their job – getting people to pay good money to run ads in the magazine – harder.

'In the end, though, all that teamwork and good feeling couldn't stop the magazine from being closed down. We had been funded by a bank that wanted to improve its image. But it was still a bank, with an eye on the "bottom line" (money). And when we were still losing money after eight years – not enough people were buying the magazine – the bank pulled the plug.'

Opposite: British typesetters in the 1920s prepare a paper for printing by setting (arranging) blocks of type which will then be printed on thousands of sheets of paper.

Carrying on the tradition

The machines that produce pages for modern newspapers and magazines are also called presses, even though computers and other new technology have replaced the old system of preparing pages by hand. Whether they are preparing a daily newspaper or a monthly magazine, every print worker knows what to do – and just as importantly, when to do it. The publication must 'go to press' by a specific time of day or night (for a daily newspaper) or by a specific date (for magazines). These deadlines cannot be moved, or the newspaper or magazine would not appear on the news-stands.

Tracing a story

Everyone working for a publication knows how they fit together as a team in the race to the printing deadline. Reporters and foreign correspondents file (send to the paper) their stories, sending them to the desk editor in charge of their department. Desk editors must decide quickly whether a story is good enough, or whether it lacks some important facts to give it real punch. They might contact the reporter or correspondent asking for more information.

When the desk editor is satisfied, copies of the story are sent – electronically today, but in the past by hand – to sub-editors and to the picture desk. The desk editor knows how many pages of the newspaper or magazine to fill, and also how much of a page any one story should occupy.

Upper and lower case type

Today, we still use the term upper case to refer to capital letters and lower case for smaller letters. These terms also date back to early printing methods. The boxes which held the metal type were called cases, and the capital letters were kept in the case above the one holding the smaller letters. Hence the names upper case and lower case.

Sub-editors edit the stories, checking the spelling and grammar (some are written in a rush). They may double-check some of the facts, or the way events are reported – publications can be sued for libel if they report inaccurately. The sub-editors make sure that the stories fit the page.

Meanwhile, picture editors look through photographs and other illustrations to find the best image to accompany the stories. Good images succeed by being dramatic, eye-catching or funny. They must also be linked to the story. At the same time, the advertising department has been filling its allocated pages with advertisements they have sold.

When all the elements of a newspaper or magazine are in place and every page has been completed according to plan, it is ready to be sent off to the printer. Journalists refer to this final stage as 'putting the paper to bed'.

SPOTLIGHT ON
The picture desk

On 12 September 2001, a day after the 9/11 terrorist attacks in the United States, newspapers around the world published what came to be known as the 'falling man' photograph. This showed a man who had jumped from the World Trade Center and fallen to his death. Picture editors, like the photographer who took the picture, believed that the image captured the human side of the tragedy. Thousands of readers, however, disagreed, and wrote angry letters to the newspapers. The photograph has rarely been seen since then.

Both photographers and passers-by witnessed the horrors of the 9/11 terrorist attack in New York City.

DIFFICULT CHOICE

Over to YOU

DO YOU THINK NEWSPAPERS WERE RIGHT TO PUBLISH THE 'FALLING MAN' PHOTOGRAPH? SHOULD SOME OF THEM BE BRAVE ENOUGH TO PUBLISH IT AGAIN NOW? SEE IF YOU CAN THINK OF SOME OF THE REASONS WHY NEWSPAPERS SHOULD – OR SHOULD NOT – BE ALLOWED TO REPRODUCE IMAGES LIKE THIS ONE.

The influence of the printed word

Nearly everyone involved with newspapers and magazines believes the saying that the pen is mightier than the sword. Many readers agree. Publications often campaign on issues – an end to an unpopular war, higher spending on schools, justice for prisoners unfairly convicted. These campaigns raise awareness about the issues and keep them in the public eye. Sometimes they help to change laws or policy.

The BLOODY MASSACRE perpetrated in King — Street BOSTON on March 5th 1770 by a party of the 29th REG.

Engrav'd Printed & Sold by PAUL REVERE BOSTON

Unhappy Boston! see thy Sons deplore,
Thy hallow'd Walks besmear'd with guiltless Gore:
While faithless P—n and his savage Bands,
With murd'rous Rancour stretch their bloody Hands;
Like fierce Barbarians grinning o'er their Prey,
Approve the Carnage and enjoy the Day.

If scalding drops from Rage from Anguish Wrung
If speechless Sorrows lab'ring for a Tongue,
Or if a weeping World can ought appease
The plaintive Ghosts of Victims such as these;
The Patriot's copious Tears for each are shed,
A glorious Tribute which embalms the Dead

But know Fate summons to that awful Goal.
Where Justice strips the Murd'rer of his Soul:
Should venal C—ts the scandal of the Land.
Snatch the relentless Villain from her Hand,
Keen Execrations on this Plate inscrib'd.
Shall reach a Judge who never can be brib'd.

The unhappy Sufferers were Mess.rs Sam.l Gray, Sam.l Maverick, Jam.s Caldwell, Crispus Attucks & Pat.k Carr
Killed. Six wounded; two of them (Christ.r Monk & John Clark) Mortally

The ability to mount such campaigns, including those that a government opposes, is one of the basic rights known as the freedom of the press. This freedom is essential to

Words and pictures can influence events and change the world forever. Before the American War of Independence, American rebels mounted anti-British protests and provoked British soldiers based there. In Boston in 1770, British soldiers fired on some local men, killing three, in a confused scuffle. The Boston Gazette *blamed the soldiers for this 'Boston Massacre', helping turn American feeling even further against Britain.*

Spotlight on
The real Private Eye

Thirteen-year-old Carl Bridgewater was shot and killed in a remote Staffordshire farmhouse in September 1978. He had apparently come across some burglars while delivering newspapers. For more than a year, Staffordshire police investigated the crime. In November 1979, four men were found guilty of murdering Carl. Michael Hickey, Vincent Hickey, Jimmy Robinson and Patrick Molloy were sent to prison for life. Michael's mother believed that the men were innocent and started a campaign for their release. Some newspapers reported this briefly, but one magazine reporter vowed to keep the campaign going. Paul Foot of *Private Eye* magazine worked for nearly 20 years to unearth information that would help the prisoners. His work succeeded. In July 1997, a court ruled that the men were wrongly convicted because the police had used false evidence to make Molloy confess. Molloy died in 1981, but the others were set free. The real murderers are still at large.

a democratic, free society in which leaders are chosen by the people and accountable to them once they are elected.

Advertising is another example of how influential newspapers and magazines can be. Companies pay to advertise their products or services. The amount depends on the size of the advertisement, ranging from whole-page or double-page ads down to much smaller ads called classifieds, which take up just a couple of lines. Placing a full-page advertisement in a national newspaper can cost more than £50,000. But that advertisement might be seen by millions of readers.

Watchdogs

It is one thing to have the freedom to influence public opinion and to make money doing so. It is quite another to abuse that freedom. Newspapers can ruin people's reputations if they print stories that

The royal blackout

Prince Harry, a second lieutenant in the army, was scheduled for active duty in Iraq in early 2007, but army officials decided against sending him. They argued that as well as facing danger himself, Harry would become a special target and endanger other soldiers. The prince was unhappy about this. Then, on 28 February 2008, the Ministry of Defence disclosed that Harry had been on front-line active service in Afghanistan since 14 December 2007. British newspapers and other media had agreed to a blackout, keeping the story secret until Harry returned safely. However, a US-based website learned of Harry's posting and announced the news. With his cover blown, Harry was sent back to the UK.

are false or deliberately misleading. Individuals can sue a publication in court for libel. If they win their case, the court may award them a large sum of money, called damages. A case usually depends on whether false printed information had a bad effect on the person's reputation. The risk of having to pay out large sums in damages if they misreport an event can make editors think twice about running stories that might be libellous.

A publication also needs to guard its reputation. Organizations nicknamed watchdogs are responsible for keeping an eye on the industry and investigating complaints. The British press operates under a system of self-regulation. This means that newspapers and magazines

Neil Kinnock had just become leader of the Labour Party in 1983 when he and his wife posed on the beach at Brighton. Film crews and photographers gleefully recorded the moment that Kinnock lost his balance and fell over – subtly casting doubt on his ability to lead.

have their own organization – independent of the government – to follow up complaints about misleading or damaging printed information. The Press Complaints Commission (PCC) deals with more than 3000 complaints and about 8500 queries every year. Editors follow a code of practice that sets standards of accuracy. The PCC investigates every complaint to check whether a newspaper or magazine has broken any rules. The bad publicity from such cases can be as damaging as an expensive libel case.

TALKING HEADS

MASS APPEAL

The *Sun* is the most widely read daily newspaper in the UK, selling about three million copies every day. It is very influential. For more than 35 years, every prime minister who has won a general election has had the support of the *Sun*. This popular tabloid paper makes no effort to hide its political opinions. Here are some of its general election headlines and the stories behind them.

'If Neil Kinnock wins today, will the last person to leave Britain please turn out the lights.' On 9 April 1992 the *Sun* predicted disaster if Labour leader Neil Kinnock defeated Conservative John Major.

'The Sun Backs Blair.' The *Sun*'s headline on 18 March 1997, at the beginning of the campaign leading up to the 1 May election (Blair faced John Major, the *Sun*'s choice in the 1992 general election).

Tabloid newspapers such as the *Sun* claim the credit for influencing the way people vote at elections, and therefore the political direction of the country. Others disagree, saying that these newspapers simply reflect, rather than change, public opinion.

News and views

Tabloid newspapers such as Britain's *Sun*, with its hard-hitting political headlines, are not the only publications that enter the world of politics and public opinion. Most serious publications have opinions and make judgements – mounting public-awareness campaigns, highlighting areas in which individuals or governments could be more generous, or simply being clear about which political parties they support.

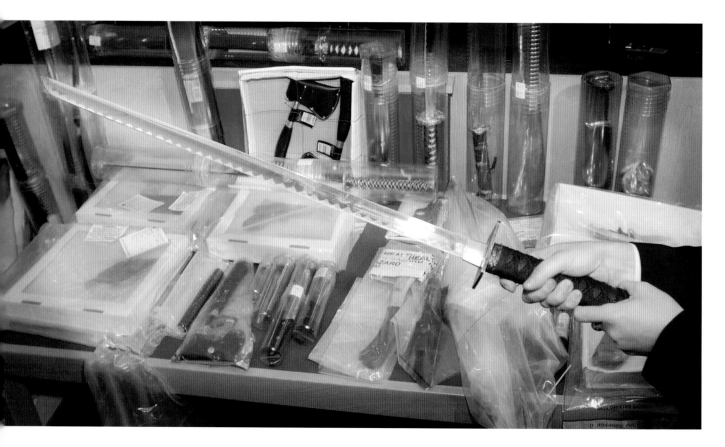

The Devon-based Express and Echo *newspaper launched a campaign to ban samurai swords like the one above after a Devon man was killed by one in 2005. Since April 2008 it has been illegal to sell, make, or hire such deadly weapons.*

FRONT-PAGE APOLOGY

Readers of Britain's *Independent on Sunday* found themselves facing an unusual front-page headline on 18 March 2007. There, taking up nearly half the page, was a massive headline reading 'Cannabis: An Apology', alongside a large photograph of a cannabis leaf.

Ten years earlier, the same newspaper had mounted a campaign to have cannabis decriminalized. It even organized a protest march in London, attracting 16,000 people. Week after week in late 1997 and beyond, the *Independent on Sunday* ran articles about how alcohol, tobacco and other legal substances were far more dangerous than cannabis. People wrote letters of support, some celebrities endorsed the campaign, and health and medical experts attended a pro-cannabis public meeting organized by the newspaper.

So the 2007 headline came as even more of a surprise to regular readers. Inside, the newspaper's editorial read: 'Yes, our front page today is calculated to grab your attention. We do not really believe that the *Independent on Sunday* was wrong at the time, ten years ago, when we called for cannabis to be decriminalized. As Rosie Boycott, who was the editor who ran the campaign, argues, the drug that she sought to decriminalize then was rather different from that which is available on the streets now.'

It went on to talk about how much more powerful – and dangerous – cannabis had become during those ten years. The paper also acknowledged newer scientific research that linked cannabis to severe mental health problems. Some people criticized the newspaper for its dramatic U-turn; others praised it for having the courage to change its mind. But amid all this argument, one thing was clear – the *Independent on Sunday*'s editorial policy on both occasions had gained publicity for the paper itself.

It is important for readers to know when a publication intends to present news objectively and when it is putting forward its own opinion. Most magazines and newspapers with an interest in politics have editorial pages. On these pages – usually two, but sometimes as many as four – most of the articles express an opinion. Some of these articles are written by regular columnists, who offer their own interpretation of current events. Readers soon come to know what sort of political opinions these columnists hold.

An editorial voice

Most prominent on the editorial pages are the editorial articles, or leaders. Newspapers usually run two or three editorials in every edition. Usually they are anonymous because they reflect the opinion of the newspaper and not that of an individual writer.

This Steve Bell cartoon appeared in the Guardian *in October 2006. It continues the tradition of mocking political leaders and their publicly-stated opinions. The words of Tony Blair, then UK prime minister, are contradicted by the fumes emitted by his 'friend', US President George W. Bush.*

SPOTLIGHT ON
Europe

Some issues create divisions in national opinion and even within political parties. During the first half of the nineteenth century, Americans could not agree on whether to continue to allow slavery and the fierce argument over this helped to trigger a civil war. For more than 35 years, the British people have debated whether the UK should play a greater role within the European Union (EU). Some people want their country to leave the EU completely.

The British press – especially some of the tabloid newspapers – has fuelled much of the anti-European opinion. Newspapers on both sides of the issue have devoted pages to detailed analysis and debate.

Others choose to stir up anti-European feeling by publicizing what they claim are ridiculous EU rules and regulations. Tabloids, especially the *Sun*, frequently run stories saying, for example, that bananas sold in the EU must have a certain shape or that the EU is causing a bra shortage. Even the broadsheet *Daily Telegraph* ran a story in 2003 claiming that EU officials were 'ready to ban yoghurt'.

READ BETWEEN THE LINES

LOOK AT A SELECTION OF NEWSPAPERS ON THE DAY AFTER A MAJOR POLITICAL EVENT, SUCH AS AN ELECTION, THE RESIGNATION OF A LEADING POLITICIAN, OR THE FIRST DAY A NEW TAX TAKES EFFECT. READ TWO CONFLICTING ACCOUNTS. IS ONE OF THEM COMPLETELY TRUE AND THE OTHER FALSE? ARE THERE GREY AREAS AROUND THE ISSUE? HOW WOULD YOU HAVE CHOSEN TO PRESENT THE STORY TO THE PUBLIC?

Over to YOU

Hold the front page

The front page of a newspaper, like the front cover of a magazine, draws the reader's eye to the main story of that particular issue. The headline, usually in larger print than anything else in the publication, might aim to shock or engage the interest of potential readers. A good headline will hook a possible reader, but stops short of telling the full story – for that the reader needs to buy the newspaper.

Some tabloid papers lead with a huge headline, coupled with an equally sensational photograph, but then tease readers by running the full story inside the newspaper. They know that many people buy papers on impulse, only if something grabs their attention. Broadsheet newspapers and magazines also use front pages as a lure, inviting potential readers to buy that issue because of the articles they will find inside.

Beaming US President Harry Truman with a copy of the newspaper which predicted that he would be defeated in the 1948 general election.

HOW NEWSPAPERS GREW

FOR DECADES, BRITISH NEWSPAPERS HAD JUST ONE SECTION. NEWS STORIES RAN FROM THE FRONT AND SPORT FROM THE BACK. BUT COMPETITION FORCED NEWSPAPER OWNERS TO FIND NEW WAYS TO ATTRACT READERS. ONE WAY WAS TO INCLUDE EXTRA SECTIONS AND MAGAZINES. IN 1962 THE *SUNDAY TIMES* PRODUCED THE UK'S FIRST COLOUR SUPPLEMENT. ITS COMPETITORS FOLLOWED, AND SOON NEWSPAPERS HAD DIFFERENT SECTIONS ON SPORT, CULTURE AND BUSINESS. BY THE END OF THE TWENTIETH CENTURY, WEEKEND EDITIONS HAD BECOME ENORMOUS AND OFTEN INCLUDED CDS, DVDS, BOOKLETS OR WALLCHARTS.

Decisions, decisions

Just what sort of story is worthy of the front page of a newspaper? Some stories, such as the terrorist attack on America on 9/11 or the death of Princess Diana, are front-page stories around the world. A newspaper would look silly or out of touch if it did not lead with these. Other front-page stories reflect the choice of the editor or even the owner of the newspaper or magazine. Some newspapers might lead with a story about a broken promise made by a politician; others (probably those which support that politician's party) will bury the story inside the paper, if they run it at all.

Newspapers often use their front pages to campaign for particular issues – they might be opposing a war, urging people to cut down on energy use or trying to slow the flow of immigrants. By whipping up support for these causes, papers hope to attract readers who share their views. Sometimes, a newspaper will mount a campaign then change its mind about the subject. Usually it simply lets the story die away once it moves on.

Facing challenges

Newspapers and magazines face many challenges as they produce issue after issue, day after day or week after week. First of all, there is the problem of deciding which stories to use and where, and how much space they should be allocated within the issue.

Reporters and photographers can sometimes face enormous obstacles in collecting up-to-date and accurate information and then transmitting it to the editorial offices on time. Over the years, readers have learned how some of the most dramatic news stories were written in the thick of battles, or in villages almost swept away by floods, or in the jungle hideouts of guerrilla leaders. In addition there is the problem of facing the representatives of

Washington Post reporters Carl Bernstein (left) and Robert Woodward uncovered the Watergate political scandal in the early 1970s. It led all the way to the office of US president Richard Nixon, who was forced to resign in 1974.

governments who do not want any bad news about their country to be reported to the outside world. News reporters face censorship, arrest and in some cases even execution for letting the world know the full story about some events.

China, the country with the largest population, has imposed restrictions on news reporting for decades. Foreign journalists are often expelled from the country for reporting news that the Chinese government does not like – about China's control of Tibet, or about injustices in the country. Chinese journalists face even harsher penalties, including fines and imprisonment for 'unofficial' (not permitted by the government) reporting of the news. In the months leading to the 2008 Olympics (hosted by China), several international organizations urged China to allow more press freedom. They pointed out that in 2001 – when the country was competing to stage the 2008 Olympics – the government promised more press freedom.

Unseen threats

Tough as all these challenges are, readers are at least aware of them. It is widely acknowledged, for example, that reporters faced enormous hardships when covering the Second World War, the 2004 Indian Ocean tsunami or life inside Saddam Hussein's Iraq. Once reports of these events or regimes were published, readers and governments could draw conclusions and decide what, if anything, they should do.

Some of the hidden obstacles for newspapers and magazines are less obvious to readers, although they may have a big effect on what news publications can print – or whether it is wise to print them at all. These obstacles may come from the government or from within the publications themselves.

Angering a president

In June 1971, while the United States was involved with the unpopular Vietnam War (see page 15), the *New York Times* and the *Washington Post* both published excerpts from the Pentagon Papers. These papers consisted of 7000 pages of top-secret US government information about the US

SPOTLIGHT ON
The deadly cartoons

On 30 September 2005, the Danish newspaper *Jyllands-Posten* published a series of 12 cartoons, some showing the Prophet Muhammad as a terrorist. Many Muslims took offence at these cartoons because their Islamic faith prohibits anyone from depicting the Prophet. The protests spread quickly from Denmark to other countries, and as a result more than 100 people died in disturbances around the world.

The cartoons had hardened people's opinions: many Muslims decided to boycott Danish products, and in some cases extended this protest to include all European goods. Some Christians living in Muslim countries faced violent threats. Meanwhile, more than 50 newspapers and magazines in Europe and the US chose to publish the cartoons – they argued that the freedom of the press was too precious to be influenced by foreign protests. The Danish prime minister echoed this opinion when he met ambassadors from Muslim countries.

Angry Jordanian Muslims burn Danish and US flags during a protest against the Jyllands-Posten *cartoons in February 2006.*

Jyllands-Posten apologized for the cartoons on 31 January 2006, but both sides in the cartoons dispute continued to stir up public opinion for nearly a year.

presence in Vietnam from 1945 to 1967. They were ideal evidence for those who disapproved of America's presence there. The government took legal action against the newspapers. Behind the scenes, President Richard Nixon said: 'people have gotta be put to the torch for this sort of thing'. The case eventually reached the Supreme Court, the highest court in America. The judges did not agree on every point, but decided that the government had no right to try to stop the papers from publishing the information. This was a victory for the freedom of the press, but some people said that similar cases in the future could be decided differently.

The bottom line?

The 'insider' challenge to news reporting comes from within news publications themselves. Imagine a newspaper has decided to publish information about how unhealthy junk food is – especially for children. Then the newspaper's advertising department tells the editor that they have sold several very expensive ads to a well-known chain of burger restaurants.

The editor knows that the extra money could pay for new offices in Tokyo or New York, or better working conditions for the editorial staff. The editor thinks that rival papers might run the same ads – getting extra money – whether or not the burger ads appear in this particular paper. Editors face this sort of decision almost every week, and readers sometimes have to decide for themselves whether the reporting of news is changed as a result.

Over to YOU

NATIONAL SECURITY?

NEWSPAPERS SOMETIMES RUN INTO TROUBLE WHEN THEY PUBLISH STORIES ABOUT GOVERNMENT FOREIGN POLICY. GOVERNMENTS ACCUSE THEM OF 'ENDANGERING NATIONAL SECURITY' BY PUBLISHING SECRETS LEAKED FROM INSIDE THE GOVERNMENT. SHOULD PUBLICATIONS BE FREE TO PUBLISH SUCH SECRETS, OR SHOULD THEY BE PREVENTED FROM CREATING PROBLEMS FOR THE GOVERNMENT?

Owning the truth?

During the 1930s and 1940s, newspapers were published every day in Nazi Germany and the Soviet Union which reported events in their own country and around the world. Many people who read these newspapers believed that they were fully informed of events, and that the German or Soviet newspapers were accurate and balanced.

We know that the press in these countries was either heavily censored or controlled by the government. Ordinary people had no way of receiving free and independent news unless they obtained smuggled copies of foreign publications or underground papers produced in their own country – at great risk to all concerned.

Moscow factory workers read about a Russian astronaut in the daily newspaper Pravda *in 1961. The communist government owned all the newspapers and controlled the information people read.*

Who makes the rules?

The UK, the United States, Australia and many other developed countries are proud of their tradition of maintaining a free press. Rather than being controlled by, or answerable to the government, newspapers and magazines can report what they please – as long as it is accurate.

But alongside this freedom is another type of influence that some people fear almost as much as outright government control. This is the influence that comes from owning newspapers or magazines. The UK has a history of strong-willed newspaper owners which goes back to the nineteenth century, when mass circulation newspapers first began to appear.

Newspaper owners such as Lord Rothermere and Lord Beaverbrook were nicknamed press barons because their influence echoed that of the English barons who forced King John to sign Magna Carta in 1215.

CHINESE WALLS

On 1 August 2007, Rupert Murdoch's News Corporation gained control of the *Wall Street Journal*, one of the world's leading financial newspapers. Earlier, Andrew Neil (who had edited the Murdoch-owned *Sunday Times* in London from 1983 to 1994) predicted how life would be at the *Journal*, based on his own experience. Here he describes a Chinese wall (an unofficial barrier) that protects editors from the views of the paper's owners. 'There's a second Chinese wall that will not survive a Murdoch takeover of the *Journal*: the barrier that ensures that what the paper writes is in no way influenced by the business interests of its owner. This seems not to exist in the Murdoch empire. Where there has been a conflict between honest journalism and Murdoch's business interests, journalism has invariably lost. I have seen this first-hand – and have even been on the receiving end.'

Editorial teams often feel pressured to echo the opinion of their bosses – or risk losing their jobs. Modern newspaper owners such as Rupert Murdoch can strengthen their influence by owning not just a number of newspapers, but television and radio networks as well. This gives someone the power to put pressure on political leaders, who know how damaging constant attacks in the press can be to their reputations.

SPOTLIGHT ON
The king of spin

Newspaper owners are not the only ones who use their power to influence the news. Politicians have always tried to make sure the press treats them well – praising them for their successes and not being too critical of their failures. More recently, high-ranking people in politics have tried to influence the information the press receives, even before newspapers can write about it. This type of filtering has become known as spin.

Alastair Campbell was Tony Blair's press secretary from 1997 to 2003. He became known as the king of spin because of the way he shaped the news. Campbell had been a journalist himself and knew how newspapers operated. From 1997 to 2000 he gave daily briefings to lobby journalists – a select group of political reporters. Campbell knew that editors were looking for snappy phrases to brighten up political stories, so he often gave them catchphrases too.

Campbell used his position to offer the government's view of important issues such as Britain's role in Europe, events in Northern Ireland, or the Iraq conflict. Sometimes this information seemed a bit one-sided, but journalists knew they might be left out of future briefings if they complained too much.

Campbell also knew how to protect his boss, the prime minister, as well as his family. Soon after Tony Blair's victory in 1997 Campbell entered 10 Downing Street (the prime minister's official home) to find the prime minister and his wife, Cherie, posing for a silly newspaper photograph. 'You can't do that!' shouted Campbell. Everyone assumed he was talking to the photographer, but his comment was, in fact, addressed to the prime minister. The photograph, Campbell had decided, was undignified and would damage Tony Blair's image.

Conrad Black (centre left) was once one of the most powerful newspaper owners in the world. He expanded his family's newspaper business to include titles in Canada, Britain and the US. But he was accused of spending company money on his expensive houses and holidays. He spent four years defending himself against dishonesty, but was eventually found guilty in an American court in 2007. He was sentenced to more than seven years in prison.

Over to YOU

LIMITING OWNERSHIP

SOME PRESS BARONS OWN DOZENS OF NEWSPAPERS AND MAGAZINES, EITHER DIRECTLY OR THROUGH COMPANIES THEY CONTROL. IS IT RIGHT THAT THESE PEOPLE, WHO HAVE NOT BEEN ELECTED TO ANY POSITION, SHOULD HAVE SO MUCH INFLUENCE? SHOULD THERE BE A LIMIT TO THE NUMBER OF PUBLICATIONS THEY OWN? CAN THERE BE SUCH A LIMIT IN A FREE SOCIETY?

Fresh faces

The world is in the midst of a communications revolution, with new – and faster – methods of sending and receiving information being introduced almost every day. The cost of this new technology is dropping, making it even easier to afford new equipment. Many of the things young people take for granted today were unknown 50 – or even 15 – years ago.

The losers in this world of instant access, high-speed change are the very media that predicted the change and recorded its arrival – newspapers and magazines. People who have grown up with satellite television, blogs, video-sharing websites and multi-use mobile phones have moved away from traditional sources of news and information. And young people make up the largest group within this trend away from the printed word.

Young Koreans in Seoul download files to their mobile phones. Asian countries such as South Korea lead the world in Internet technology, which many experts see as the future of newspapers.

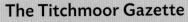

The Titchmoor Gazette

TeacherNet, a UK government-funded educational website, offers classes the chance to view and discuss how a newspaper works with a special Flash Player application. This in-depth look at a typical – but imaginary – regional newspaper breaks down the process of putting the paper together into 12 clear-cut steps. Along the way, children can stop and discuss the problems faced, and solved, by the different teams working for the *Titchmoor Gazette*. This is like being right on the scene, as the issue moves from the planning stage (a busy editorial meeting) through reporting, late-breaking news, gathering advertising, sub-editing, finding photographs, printing and sending out the 160,000 copies to newsagents.

Young people needed

On the other hand, the decline in young people's interest in newspapers and magazines could have some positive effects – at least on people setting out on their careers. With fewer young people being associated with printed news, those who are interested could find it much easier to make their mark. The alternative – a younger generation which is not involved in the media in any way – could have wider consequences. Without a vigorous press to watch over them, governments can become lazy or, in extreme cases, corrupt. Martin P. Wattenberg, an expert on American politics, believes that if young people continue to be under-represented in the press, the result could be 'a government of old people, by old people, and for old people'.

Carrying on a tradition

Those young people who do take advantage of new openings know that they are continuing a long tradition. And this is not a dull and dusty tradition such as the tradition of knowing how to address a letter to a lord or deciding which piece of cutlery to use. It is the tradition of dissent, protest and bringing about real changes in society. Young people in most countries are being urged to take more part in the democracies that govern their lives. Simply bothering to vote can be a step in that direction, but gathering – and reporting – news and expressing thought-out political opinions is even more inspiring.

Taking part in student debates can be excellent preparation for becoming a columnist in later life. Working on a student newspaper or magazine can teach young people the skills needed to produce a news publication. Just as importantly, this experience can help them learn to read about the wider world. Being able to sense what a paper chooses not to write – or feels it cannot write – gives people a huge advantage.

Newspapers and magazines are evolving fast in response to modern communications techniques for news-gathering and production. Young people can apply their technical knowledge in this new environment, which may help to give them a head start in their career.

Journalism teacher Jan Gottschalk helps students in Carrboro, North Carolina, USA, produce the first edition of their school newspaper using the latest computer design technology.

SPOTLIGHT ON
Young reporters

Even the largest newspapers, which have permanent reporters in cities around the world, rely on news agencies for some of their stories. News agencies are organizations of journalists which pool their information to provide news about events around the world. They then sell their stories to newspapers, television and radio networks, and other companies.

In 1975, a new type of news agency began operating from offices in New York City. Called Children's Express, it used researchers, reporters and editors who were all aged between eight and eighteen. The agency worked like other news agencies: researchers found out about newsworthy stories, reporters researched the latest information and editors worked on the finished stories to make sure they were accurate and read well. Most importantly, Children's Express sold stories to leading newspapers and other media companies.

Children's Express set up a British branch in 1994, operating along similar lines to the original. In 2007, it changed its name to Headliners. Since then it has been a real success – more than 1200 stories have been prepared for publication and 2500 young people have been introduced to journalism. Headliners stories span a range of subjects; many deal with troubling or difficult issues. Recent stories have focused on people with disabilities, lingering divisions in Northern Ireland and gun crime.

TALKING HEADS

'I think I have changed a lot. I feel I am more confident, more able to communicate properly with others and more knowledgeable about reporting, technology and the working world in general.'

Clare, 17 years old, discussing her involvement with Headliners.

The shape of the future

Faced with competition from the Internet, 24-hour TV news stations and new applications for mobile phones, newspapers and magazines face difficult times. British newspaper circulation figures paint a gloomy picture. Only one national newspaper – the *Financial Times* – increased readership during 2007. Others lost up to six per cent of readers in that period.

The United States has less of a tradition of national newspapers, but its newspaper readership has also declined. In the year ending 30 April 2007, 14 of the top 20 newspapers in the US lost readers.

Not all gloom and doom

The news is not all bad. Successful new publications are being introduced throughout much of the developing world. The World Association of Newspapers notes that the number of newspapers sold daily in India rose by a third between 2001 and 2005. Brazil, another huge developing country, also had a thriving newspaper industry over that period. Of the top 100 highest-selling newspapers in the world, 60 are produced in China, Japan and India. Much of this increase comes from

A mountain of newspapers awaits recycling. Will newspapers survive in the 'paperless society' of the future?

In 2006, the *British Journalism Review* (*BJR*) conducted a survey to see how much people's reading habits had changed over the previous two years. It asked people whether they read a newspaper more often, less often or about the same as they did two years before. More than half answered 'about the same', but three times as many people said they read papers less often than those who read more often.

The *BJR* then asked why people read papers less – or more – often. The biggest reasons for decline were that people could find the same information elsewhere, that they no longer had time to read newspapers and that they could not rely on papers to be fair and accurate. However, readers still felt that they could find more national and local news in their newspapers than from other sources.

cheaper printing costs. This same drop in the real cost of publishing has led to the growth of another type of publication in Britain and other countries – free newspapers. These are delivered free in a neighbourhood or in easy-to-see display cases in towns and cities. They cover the cost of producing and distributing their papers solely by selling advertisements. Many of these free sheets make good profits.

LOOKING AHEAD

WHAT DO YOU THINK ARE THE MOST PROMISING – AND CHALLENGING – ASPECTS OF PRINT JOURNALISM OVER THE NEXT TEN YEARS? IS THE AGE OF INK-ON-PAPER PRINTING OVER, AS SOME PEOPLE HAVE SUGGESTED? AND IF IT IS NOT, WHAT SPECIAL ADVANTAGES DO PRINTED NEWSPAPERS AND MAGAZINES HAVE OVER 'VIRTUAL' VERSIONS OF THE NEWS?

Over to YOU

Glossary

allies   Countries that join forces during a war.

boycott   To refuse to buy goods or services as a way of making a protest.

briefing   A meeting to pass information from the government to reporters.

circulation   The number of copies a newspaper or magazine sells.

coalition   A group of organizations or countries joining together for a shared aim.

code of practice   A set of rules on how to do a certain job.

columnist   Someone who writes a regular article (column) in a newspaper or magazine.

Congress   The elected law-making branch of the US government, like a parliament.

contradictory   So different as to be almost opposite.

correspondent   A reporter who specializes in a subject (such as education or law) or one who is based in another city or country.

corrupt   Dishonestly using a position to gain an advantage.

decriminalize   Reduce the legal penalties against.

desk   A newspaper and magazine term to describe a department.

dissent   Strong disagreement about or disapproval of something.

editorial   An article in which a newspaper or magazine offers its own opinion.

embedded journalist   A reporter who is assigned to accompany a particular group of soldiers during a conflict.

excerpt   A short section of a book, long article or letter.

grey area   A situation with no clear rules.

guerrilla   A member of an unofficial military group that uses surprise attacks.

hoax   A plan to trick or deceive.

lead story   The most prominent story on the front page of a newspaper.

leader   Another term for an editorial article.

leaked   Secretly passed on information to the press.

libel   An untruth about someone that is printed.

Nazi   The political party that led Germany to cause the Second World War.

Saddam Hussein   A brutal leader of Iraq who was arrested in 2003 and executed in 2006.

scoop   An exciting news story that one newspaper prints before any of its rivals.

Second World War   The war from 1939 to 1945 between Germany, Japan, Italy and their allies against the UK, the United States, China and their allies.

sub-editor Someone who works on articles to make sure they are accurate and fit the space planned for them.

sued Started a legal case in court against an individual or company.

tsunami A massive wave caused by an earthquake on the ocean floor.

underground Unofficial and illegal.

Vietnam War The war from 1959 to 1975 in which American armed forces tried – and eventually failed – to stop the North Vietnamese army from defeating the South Vietnamese.

woodblock A form of printing in which an image is carved on to the surface of a piece of wood, which is then covered with ink so the image can be stamped on to a page.

Further reading

Newspapers, Behind the Media series, Catherine Chambers (Heinemann Library, 2001)

Books and Newspapers, Communications Close-up series, Ian Graham (Evans, 2003)

Newspapers, Communicating Today series, Chris Oxlade (Heinemann Library, 2002)

Newspapers, Media series, Michael and Jane Pelusy (Chelsea House, 2005)

Newspapers and Magazines, Mediawise series, Julian Petley (Hodder Wayland 2002)

Website links

Headliners

http://www.headliners.org/

Media Awareness Network

http://www.media-awareness.ca/

The Newspaper Society

http://www.newspapersoc.org.uk/

Titchmoor Gazette

www.teachnet-uk.org.uk/.../newspaper_simulation/
Day_in_the_life_of_the_Titchmoor_Gazette.htm

Index